AUSTRALIAN TROPICAL
Orchids

Bill Lavarack & Bruce Gray

Dendrobium bigibbum var. compactum

Published in Australia
by FRITH & FRITH Books
"Prionodura" P.O. Box 581,
Malanda, Queensland 4885
Telephone (070) 96 8105
Facsimile (070) 96 8316

National Library of Australia
Card Number ISBN 0 9589942 8 5

First printed 1992

Other books in this series:

Australian Tropical Birds
Australian Tropical Reptiles and Frogs
Australian Tropical Reef Life
Australian Tropical Butterflies
Australia's Cape York Peninsula
Australia's Wet Tropics Rainforest Life

Dendrobium speciosum

Rhinerrhiza moorei

Preface

One hundred and eight orchids are illustrated in this book, a little less than half the species in the north-eastern part of Queensland. Some are well known, spectacular species, but a few are much less common and in fact about six of the illustrations in this book represent the first publication of a photograph of a species. The species have been chosen to illustrate a range of the variation in plant size, form and habitat present in the Australian tropics. In some the whole plant is shown and an impression of the habitat is given, while in others a close up of the detail of the flowers has been used.

Many of the photographs were taken in the natural habitat. In a few cases, particularly in the case of close ups, the plants have been photographed indoors in studio conditions as some flowers are tiny and perfect light and still conditions are necessary to get a good result.

Our interest in orchids goes back over thirty years. During that period we have been fortunate to have made many trips to Cape York Peninsula, both for our work as professional scientists and simply for our love of the Peninsula and its orchids. These trips have been interspersed with numerous shorter trips in the Wet Tropics region which is on our doorstep. This has lead to the discovery of about thirty species new to science and several new records for Australia. Few experiences can match the excitement of the discovery of a new orchid species in some remote corner of the Peninsula.

Very few of tropical Australia's orchids have common names. Often where there is a common name it applies to different species in different regions and confusion can easily arise. Over the years amateur orchid enthusiasts have tended to use the scientific names especially for less common and sometimes small, easily-overlooked species which are so rarely discussed by people other than orchid specialists that common names have not been coined.

The scientific names of many Australian orchids are currently in a period of uncertainty. New ideas which dramatically increase the number of species by splitting up established ones are being debated as this book goes to press. The names used in this book represent the views of the authors on this matter and have been formulated as a result of many years of field experience. A largely conservative approach has been taken in these pages and the splitting of well known species such as the King Orchid, the Cooktown Orchid and the Tea Tree Orchid have not been accepted as the authors believe the similarities in these species outweigh the differences.

Bill Lavarack

Bruce Gray

Introduction

What is an orchid?

To many people the word "orchid" is associated with adjectives such as "exotic" or "rare" or "delicate", but Australian orchids answer to none of these labels. The orchid family is, in fact, a group of very hardy plants and a very abundant group in the wild. They belong to the Orchidaceae, which, according to some authorities, is the largest of the plant families.

In the tropics of north-eastern Australia there are some 230 orchid species, between one quarter and one third of Australia's orchids. They have evolved to thrive in a variety of niches, showing the following life forms: growing on trees ("epiphytes"); on rocks ("lithophytes"); in the ground ("terrestrials"). Some terrestrial species have lost the chlorophyll and the ability to derive energy from sunlight, relying on symbiotic fungi in the soil to provide food. These species are known as "saprophytes".

The orchids are characterised by the recurring themes of animal pollination and wind dispersal and it is the adaptations to these two ends, in particular to the former, which give the orchids their common features. To achieve efficient pollination, the pollen grains are massed into discrete parcels (pollinia) which are readily carried around by insects. But to entice or trick the insect into doing this, the orchids have evolved flowers which, to the human eye, are sometimes spectacularly beautiful, sometimes rather dull, occasionally weird but, to the student of nature, always interesting. The orchid flower consists of the following parts: three sepals which are similar and are radially arranged; three petals, one of which is usually highly modified to attract the insect pollinators and often provides a landing platform; in the centre of the flower the male and female parts of the flower are fused into a column with the single anther at the end. The column and lip are typical of most orchids. In a few species the lip is designed to mimic a female insect and attracts the unsuspecting male to attempt to mate with it. The colours, shapes and scents used to attract insects are seemingly endless and in this lies much of the attraction of the orchids to the human observer.

A few of Australia's orchids are truly spectacular, none more so than the Cooktown Orchid (see pages 4, 46 and 47) which has been ranked among the world's most attractive species. The large, delicately-coloured pink flowers are still a common sight in the Cape York Peninsula monsoon scrubs. Another attractive and extremely common species is the Golden Orchid (see page 7) which is a feature of coastal scrubs and mangroves from Gladstone to New Guinea. Along with these and a few other large, attractive species are scores of smaller species which are often overlooked, but are always rewarding to the nature lover. To see these the orchid enthusiast often has to leave the shade of the rainforests and venture into less "fashionable" habitats such as the Tea Tree forests of the coastal plain. Here, amidst the almost unbearable humidity and the mosquitos of the tropical wet season, the diligent searcher will find between ten and twenty orchid species, one or two spectacular, but all beautiful in their own way.

The Australian Tropics as Orchid Habitats

The Wet Tropics and the Cape York Peninsula area of north-eastern Queensland are two of the most diverse biological regions in Australia. Both are areas of reliable high, but seasonal rainfall.

The Wet Tropics comprise the coastal ranges and the narrow coastal plain between Townsville and Cooktown. Orchids are abundant from the rainforests, open forests and mangroves of the hot humid coast to the cool, misty cloud forests of the mountain tops and even in the tall, eucalypt-dominated forests of the western fall of the ranges. It is this diversity in habitats which has resulted in the rich diversity in orchids.

Separated from the Wet Tropics by the dry, low-lying Laura Basin are the more seasonal forests of Cape York Peninsula. Here the mountains are lower and the main diversity lies in rainfall patterns and soils. The best of the Peninsula's rainforests, such as those of the McIlwraith Range, are almost as well developed as those in the Wet Tropics, but much of the Peninsula is more seasonal, having to contend with a regular drought each year from May to December. Surprisingly, many orchids have adapted to cope with these conditions and upwards of 100 species have been recorded from Cape York Peninsula, although most occur in the rainforests and monsoon forests of the northern and eastern parts.

In this book the Wet Tropics have been subdivided into lowland and upland types, each of which has then been further divided into rainforests and open forests. Cape York Peninsula has been divided into rainforests and open forests. The Cape York Peninsula open forests have here been taken to include deciduous vine thickets. All this may sound neat and precise, but nothing is so simple in nature, and many of the orchids occur in more than one of these habitat types.

Conservation

The beauty and fascination of the orchids have inevitably led to a desire by people to collect them. In some cases this collecting has resulted in a significant decrease in orchid numbers. Many, perhaps most, of the collected plants die soon after collection. People being what they are, it seems unlikely that this desire to collect orchids will disappear, although the orchids may if we are not careful. There are different ways of approaching the problem and one that could work is to ensure that the more sought after plants are available from artificially-propagated nursery stock.

Naturally-occurring populations will need protection and this can be afforded to some extent by National Parks and the World Heritage Area, although it must be recognised that simply declaring an area as National Park does not protect the plants in it. As well as regular ranger patrols, there needs to be strong legislation which not only makes it illegal to remove plants, but also makes it illegal to trade in any which have been illegally obtained.

There is nothing wrong with growing native orchids, in fact it often leads to an increased awareness of nature and can provide a reserve of plants if other conservation measures fail. However there are a few simple rules which should be followed:
(1) be fully aware of the legislation regarding collecting from the wild;
(2) never collect unless you have the permission of the owner of the land; (3) only collect from areas which have been, or are to be, cleared; (4) do not buy native orchids unless you are satisfied that they were legally obtained originally; (5) do not collect or purchase plants which you do not have the expertise or the conditions to grow successfully; (6) do not collect more than you need for yourself.

Dendrobium smillieae

WET TROPICS LOWLAND OPEN FORESTS

Open forests (**right**) occur in the wet lowlands on areas of poor soils, on poorly-drained sites or on fire-prone sites. There are several intergrading types including those dominated by eucalypts and those dominated by melaleucas. A large proportion of the coastal lowlands has been cleared for sugar cane, pine plantations or grazing.

The open eucalypt forests of the coastal strip are moist habitats, often with rainforest-related understorey which varies in development in relation to recent fire history. In moister areas and along the numerous small watercourses are a variety of trees such as Red Beech, *Dillenia alata*, and Swamp Box, *Lophostemon suaveolens*, which are suited to epiphytic orchids. Terrestrial species also occur, many flowering immediately after the first soaking rains of the wet season.

The melaleuca forests and woodlands are developed on poorly-drained soils and are often virtually pure stands of the Broad-leaved Tea Tree, *Melaleuca viridiflora*. The effects of the dry season are pronounced in this habitat and all the orchids exhibit adaptations to cope with the dry months from June to December. The terrestrial species weather the harsh conditions and regular fires of the dry season as underground tubers and several species of *Habenaria* are present along with a variety of other genera. Most of these are wet season flowerers, ranging from late November to April. The Tea Tree Orchid, *Dendrobium canaliculatum* (see page 9), with its swollen stems and thick leathery leaves is the only epiphyte which is well adapted to these forests.

Dwarf Cooktown Orchid
Dendrobium bigibbum var. *compactum*

There is much debate over the status of this attractive dwarf form of the Cooktown Orchid, but one thing is certain – it is one of the most beautiful of north Queensland's orchids (**page ii**). It has been recorded from the Macalister Range between Cairns and the Mossman River and possibly from a few other peaks in the general region. It grows almost exclusively on rocks in exposed situations, fortunately in some inaccessible positions. The rainfall here is considerably above that which is typical of the areas where Cooktown Orchids grow on Cape York Peninsula. This variety maintains its dwarf habit even when grown in cultivation, while many other allegedly dwarf forms from further north do not, suggesting that this is genetically distinct to some extent.

The Dwarf Cooktown Orchid is an excellent variety for cultivation, but must be given perfect drainage. It has been heavily collected and while populations remain on cliff faces, it must be regarded as endangered.

Bottle Brush Orchid
Dendrobium smillieae

The Bottle Brush Orchid is named for the tightly-bunched flower spike (**page 3**). It occurs from Mount Elliot to the islands of Torres Strait and New Guinea where it is an abundant species. It is predominantly a species of open, lowland coastal habitats. Although it also occurs in rainforests, it is more common in moist open forests and rainforest margins, being equally at home on trees or rocks. The plant size is variable with stems up to one metre long, but commonly half that. The flowers are about two centimetres long and are variable with various colour combinations of pink, green and white. The main flowering time is July to October and the flowers are moderately long-lasting.

This is a good species for cultivation, doing well in a pot or on a tree in tropical or subtropical Queensland gardens, but needs to be kept moist year round. It is not under any threat.

Black Orchid
Cymbidium canaliculatum

This hardy species (**left above**) grows in country where no other orchid can survive. It is an epiphyte of the drier open forests of northern Australia. It grows high up in ironbarks and other eucalypts well above the reach of fires, often in the hollows of dead limbs. Here the roots penetrate long distances into the cool moist decomposing wood, where they are protected from the harsh, dry conditions of the inland open forests. The flowers are two to four centimetres across and are variable in colour, ranging from pale green, through light brown to dark brown and purple. Flowering is during late spring.

This is not an easy plant to grow in cultivation. Many plants suffer severe damage during collection due to the long and well-attached root system. In cultivation it requires a perfectly drained medium and a dry season. Although much habitat has been cleared, this is still a very abundant species and is under no threat.

Snake Orchid
Cymbidium suave

An epiphyte of open forests, this species (**left**) occurs in eastern Australia from south-eastern New South Wales to near Cooktown. It grows in coastal and subcoastal open forests at sea level to 1000 metres, in hollow dead branches where the fleshy roots penetrate into the rotting wood. The flowers are about two to three centimetres across and, as the scientific name suggests, are fragrant. The flowering season in the tropics is August to October. The long stems are unusual for the genus and may grow up to half a metre in length.

The Snake Orchid does well in cultivation, but many collected plants die as they do not withstand damage well and extreme care is needed in transplanting larger plants. This species is not regarded as being under any threat.

Blue Beards
Calochilus caeruleus

This is one of the "bearded orchids", so named for the prominent hairs on the labellum (**left**). It is a small terrestrial species which occurs across the monsoonal country at the top of Australia, and the islands of Torres Strait and southern New Guinea. It is a species of the melaleuca forests of coastal and subcoastal areas at low altitudes. These habitats are inundated during the annual wet season in summer and autumn, then often suffer seasonal drought for the rest of the year. The plants survive the dry season as underground tubers and produce a flower spike after the first soaking rains in about January. The flowers are about one and a half centimetres across and usually only one or two are open at one time, however the inflorescence opens progressively and is in flower for about five or six weeks.

This species is difficult to maintain in cultivation for more than a year or two. In the Wet Tropics the habitat has been extensively cleared and the species is under some pressure there. However in other areas the species appears to be reasonably secure.

Golden Orchid
Dendrobium discolor

The Golden Orchid (**opposite above**) grows in coastal Queensland from about Gladstone to the islands of Torres Strait and New Guinea. It is a species of more open habitats such as coastal rockfaces, open forests, mangroves, beach scrubs and rainforest margins. The long-lasting flowers are about five or six centimetres across, ranging from chocolate brown to yellow and are borne in long sprays in July to October. The plant can be extremely large with some canes reaching five metres. The stems produce large numbers of aerial growths which start up a new plant wherever they touch rocks, producing large colonies.

It is an excellent species for horticulture, doing well in gardens at least as far south as Brisbane. Never entirely satisfactory in a pot, this species does best tied to a tree in a well lit position. Although heavily collected in the wild, this species is under no immediate threat as large numbers remain in many locations.

Yellow Golden Orchid
Dendrobium discolor
var. *broomfieldii*

This most attractive orchid (**opposite below**) is actually a Golden Orchid which is missing a pigment from the flower, resulting in a brilliant yellow, rather than the normal golden brown. Occasional plants have been found in most areas where the Golden Orchid grows, but observations have been even more common in the Whitsunday Islands – perhaps because there are so many Golden Orchids there and they are so readily seen from a boat. The brilliant yellow flowers are about five centimetres across and stand out from the brown forms which surround it.

This variety is in demand and is collected heavily whenever word gets out about a new locality.

Kurrimine Elbow Orchid
Arthrochilus dockrillii

Named after one of Australia's most respected orchid botanists, Alick Dockrill, this small terrestrial species **(right)** occurs from about Cardwell to the tip of Cape York Peninsula, the islands of Torres Strait and probably in New Guinea. It grows in the coastal lowlands in open forests dominated by *Melaleuca* or *Eucalyptus* species on sandy soil. It forms large loose colonies, but usually only a few plants are in flower at any time. The flowers are about one and a half centimetres across, and are long-lasting. The flowers appear weird to the human eye, but are designed to mimic a female insect and trick the male into attempting to mate and, in doing so, effect pollination. The leaves appear soon after the start of the wet season and the flowers are borne spasmodically from then to spring. The single, linear leaf is usually present at flowering, but dies off during the dry season.

This species is amenable to cultivation, but requires a dry resting period during winter and spring. It is not under significant threat, although much suitable habitat has been cleared in the southern part of the range.

Crystal Bells
Didymoplexis pallens

Finding this tiny terrestrial species **(right)** usually means getting down on hands and knees in soggy melaleuca forests where it is hidden in the grass and sedges. It occurs on the east Queensland coast from about Cardwell to Cairns and probably on Cape York Peninsula. It also occurs on the islands of Torres Strait and near Darwin and also is widespread in the Indonesian and Malaysian Islands and South East Asia. It is a saprophyte, lacking any leaves or green tissue and living as an underground tuber all year until the flowering occurs during the wet season, usually in December to March. In the melaleuca and eucalypt forests around Cardwell it is actually quite common, but is rarely seen because of the small size and the brief flowering period and ephemeral nature of the flowers. On one occasion in December, not long after the first heavy rains of the season, one of the authors happened on an area that had been burnt a few months previously and the forest floor was dotted with the glistening white one centimetre wide flowers of this delightful miniature species. After pollination the pedicel extends, elevating the seed capsule above the ground to give the tiny seeds a better chance of being dispersed on the wind.

The species cannot be grown in cultivation and therefore there is no collecting pressure on the populations. Although the known habitat of this species in Queensland is under pressure, there are good populations remaining in at least two national parks.

Habenaria propinquior

The upright, white spikes of this attractive, small terrestrial (**left**) are a common wet season sight in open forests from Rockhampton to the tip of Cape York Peninsula and the islands of Torres Strait and, probably, southern parts of New Guinea. It grows in open forests and even more commonly in woodlands dominated by the Broad-leaved Tea Tree, *Melaleuca viridiflora*, in sandy soil. These habitats are inundated every summer, but are dry from about early winter to early summer each year. The leaves appear soon after the first soaking rains each year in December or January and the flowers follow about a month later, if the rainfall has been sufficient, and last for about a month or so. During the dry winter and spring the leaves wither and the plants survive as underground tubers. The flowers are about eight millimetres across.

This is an abundant species which is easy to grow if given the correct dry periods. It is not considered to be under any threat, although the habitat in some areas has been depleted by clearing.

Tea Tree Orchid
Dendrobium canaliculatum

The Tea Tree Orchid (**left**) is one of the most widespread of tropical Australian orchids, occurring from Gladstone to the tip of Cape York Peninsula, the islands of Torres Strait to southern New Guinea, Northern Territory and the Kimberley region of Western Australia. As might be expected from a species covering such a wide area, this is a variable species with at least three varieties being recognized. Different colour combinations of brown, white, purple and yellow occur in different regions, leading some authorities to split the Tea Tree Orchid into three separate species. The flowers are about two centimetres across. Forests of the Broad-leaved Tea Tree, *Melaleuca viridiflora*, are often thickly populated with this compact, colourful orchid which flowers from August to November. The swollen stems and leaves are an adaptation to the harsh dry winter and spring of the tropics. The paperbark forests are subject to regular fires and tea tree orchids always grow high in the trees where these fires cannot reach.

The species can be cultivated successfully, but often its commonness leads to carelessness and most collected plants survive only for a year or two. Although a relatively abundant species, numbers are dwindling in some areas from the twin threats of collecting and land clearing, as large tracts of tea tree forest between Mackay and Cairns disappear. It is not regarded as threatened in the short term.

Red Beech Orchid
Eria fitzalanii

One of the more common epiphytes of the lowlands, the delicate, perfumed flowers **(right)** adorn moister open forests from Mount Elliot near Townsville to the tip of Cape York Peninsula and the islands of Torres Strait. It is most common in lowland moist open forests, but also occurs in rainforest situations where there is good light, and it extends to about 1000 metres in altitude. It often prefers trees with a papery or flaky bark such as Swamp Box, *Lophostemon suaveolens*, and Red Beech, *Dillenia alata*. The flowers are about one and a half centimetres across and are borne in spring (August to October). This is a common species in the coastal lowland open forests between Townsville and Cooktown and at Iron Range and the Bamaga area.

It is a good species in cultivation, doing well in a small pot of well drained medium, or on a tree in a tropical garden. In the southern part of its range it is suffering from extensive land clearing, but it is not threatened as a species.

Habenaria rumphii

The densely-packed, glistening white spikes of flowers of this beautiful small terrestrial species **(right)** are reasonably rare in Australia. It has been recorded from a few localities between Cardwell and Iron Range on the tropical Queensland coast, in the northern part of the Northern Territory and on the islands of Torres Strait. It is also a widespread species outside Australia, occurring in New Guinea, Indonesia and South East Asia. It is a species of grassy open forests and grasslands, usually in rich loamy soil. The plants are seasonal, with the leaves appearing soon after the first soaking rains each year in December or January and the flowers following about a month later and lasting about a month or so. During the dry winter and spring the leaves wither and the plants survive as underground tubers. The flowers are about one centimetre across and are borne in late summer (February to March). In Australia it was previously known as *Habenaria holtzei*.

This species is rewarding in cultivation if given a dry resting period during winter and spring. It is not a common species in Australia, but is not considered to be under any threat.

Nervilia plicata

The distinctive, ribbed, hairy leaves which lie
flat on the ground in large colonies are a feature of
tropical open forests, but the flowers (**left**) of this
orchid are very rarely seen. It is a small terrestrial
species which occurs from Rockhampton to the tip
of Cape York Peninsula, the Top End of the Northern
Territory, the islands of Torres Strait, New Guinea,
Indonesia and South East Asia. It grows in moister
open forests and rainforest margins, in good, well
drained soil from the lowlands to about 1000 metres
in altitude. The plants survive the long dry season as
underground tubers. When the first storm rain falls
in December, it initiates the flowering. The leaves
follow later and eventually die off in the dry season
during late winter. The flowers are about five
centimetres across and last a few days. This species
grows in large colonies, but plants appear to flower
only occasionally when the season is right.

It does well in cultivation if grown in a rich well
drained mixture. It is not under any threat.

Malaxis latifolia

The light green, glossy, pleated leaves (**left**)
are the most attractive feature of this species
as the flowers are tiny – about six millimetres across.
It is one of the common terrestrial species of north
Queensland from Mount Elliot near Townsville to
the tip of Cape York Peninsula through the islands
of Torres Strait to New Guinea, Indonesia, Malaysia
and South East Asia to Japan. In Australia this
species grows at low to moderate altitudes in
rainforests and moister open forests, but always in
shady, protected situations where there is a good
accumulation of leaf litter. Occasional large plants
up to half a metre are seen, but plants more
commonly grow to about twenty five centimetres
tall. The plant is deciduous losing it's leaves in the
dry season and growing new leaves with the onset
of the wet. The flowers are also produced during
the wet (January to April).

It is a good subject for cultivation in a well
drained mixture and makes a good foliage plant
if the grower can forgive it the deciduous season.
It is an abundant species and is under no threat.

WET TROPICS LOWLAND RAINFORESTS

The lowlands are confined to the narrow coastal strip between Townsville and Cooktown. Not all of this is rainforest, in fact more than half was originally open forest and a large proportion is now cleared. Lowland rainforests are often heavily cyclone-damaged and feature many wattles in their canopies. This tends to be a rather poor orchid habitat with a limited number of species present. However things are very different in the forests fringing the major streams **(right)**. Here the creek or river bed forms a wind tunnel and air movement is consequently high, as are light penetration and humidity levels. These conditions lead to concentrations of epiphytes both in the canopy and quite low down on tree trunks and rocks, although above normal flood level.

Mangroves occur along stream estuaries and on sheltered sections of coastline. Although not large in area, the mangroves are a very rich orchid habitat in areas where the rainfall is high. This richness in the mangroves is not surprising as the mangroves essentially are extensions of the rainforest particularly as far as conditions in the canopy are concerned. Humidity is always high in the mangroves, but most of the forest comprises a single species unsuited to epiphytes and consequently has few orchids. As in other rainforests it is the margins of the mangrove forests which are rich in orchid species as there is a greater diversity of tree species and better light and air movement.

Moth Orchid
Phalaenopsis rosenstromii

The Moth Orchid is sometimes also locally known as the Mount Spec Orchid after the mountain near Townsville which marks the southern limit of this species. It occurs spasmodically along the Queensland coast to the Iron Range area on Cape York Peninsula and also in New Guinea. It is a species of the lowland gorges, usually growing in shady conditions mostly on trees or vines, but occasionally on rocks. When not in flower the plants can be very difficult to see, and plants are often detected by means of the vigorous root system which may extend metres from the plant. The conditions are always humid and even in winter low temperatures are rare. The large spectacular flowers **(back cover)** are-long lasting, about five centimetres across, and are borne on branched inflorescences up to forty centimetres long. The main flowering is during the wet season (December to March), but can occur at almost any time. This species is one of the finest and most sought after of the world's orchids, being a parent of countless hybrids.

It does well in cultivation provided the warm moist year-round climate can be duplicated in a bushhouse or glasshouse. While the habitats are rarely cleared, the Moth Orchid is under pressure from collectors as it is such a fine horticultural subject and is now considered vulnerable in Australia.

Aphyllorchis anomala

This small leafless species (**left**) is very rarely seen as it is below ground except for the brief period when in flower. It is restricted to the Wet Tropics between Cooktown and Babinda, where it apparently grows at low altitudes in rainforest conditions. It has been recorded in small colonies near stream banks in organically rich soil. The flowering is spasmodic throughout the year, possibly in reaction to rainfall. The flowers are numerous, about one and a half centimetres across and last a week. The flowering stem is up to a metre tall. It is a saprophytic species, meaning that it lacks chlorophyll and obtains its food requirements from fungi in the soil.

The saprophytic lifeform makes it virtually impossible to grow in cultivation. It has been listed as a "poorly known" species, but it is never collected and much of the habitat remains in areas such as the Daintree River National Park and Cape Tribulation National Park, so that it is unlikely to be under threat.

Bulbophyllun baileyi

The long climbing stems of this species often form a dense mat on tree trunks and rock faces, particularly near creeks in the Wet Tropics (see habitat picture on page 54, tree on left). It is a familiar sight in rainforests from about Mount Elliot near Townsville to the tip of Cape York Peninsula, and the islands of Torres Strait and New Guinea. It is a species of rainforests, rainforest margins and moister open forests from sea level to moderate altitudes and is one of the north's most widespread species. It will tolerate deep shade or full sunlight, although it does not flower well in shady conditions. The flowers (**left**) are quite large for a *Bulbophyllum* species (about four centimetres across) and are sweetly scented but last only a few days. They are produced singly but a large plant may have several open at one time. The flowering season is spasmodic and flowers may be present at any time of the year.

This species does well in cultivation but its wandering growth makes it unsuited to a pot, and a slab or tree is best. This is an abundant species and under no threat from collectors or land clearing.

Caterpillar Orchid
Cheirostylis ovata

It is easy to overlook this tiny terrestrial species **(right)** as it is often covered with leaf debris on the forest floor. It grows in moist environments from north-eastern New South Wales to the Iron Range area on Cape York Peninsula. It invariably grows in shady conditions, usually within rainforests but occasionally in moist open forests, but not in areas where fires occur. In the tropics it grows from sea level to about 700 metres altitude. It commonly grows on rocks where there is some accumulation of leaf litter and the drainage is perfect, but may also grow in leaf litter on the forest floor. The fleshy stems are a feature of this species as they tend to be swollen between the nodes and have numerous root hairs attaching the plant to the rock or to a leaf. The flowers are about one centimetre long and are produced in winter-spring. Two or three flowers are usually open at a time. The leaves are about two to four centimetres long and are delicately veined and quite attractive. They are deciduous, withering when conditions become drier in winter and spring.

It is rarely grown, but does well in a shallow pot of leaf mould if not over watered. It is under no threat in the wild.

Malaxis lawleri

Known from one location only, this small terrestrial species **(right)** occurs in the ranges south of Cooktown at moderate elevation. The only known populations are growing on the bank of a creek and an associated pandanus swamp in shaded, moist conditions. The flowers are about six millimetres across and are borne on a flowering stem up to ten centimetres tall with five to ten flowers which last about two weeks. The flowering season appears to be December to February. It is the smallest of the Australian species of *Malaxis*, being only about four or five centimetres tall. The leaves are about four centimetres long and are deciduous, withering in winter with new leaves being produced in the wet season.

This species has proved easy to grow, but it is extremely rare and none should be collected in the wild other than as part of an officially approved attempt to preserve the species in cultivation. The habitat is severely disturbed by feral pigs which dig up the swamp and there is only a limited number of plants of this species left in the area. It is regarded as endangered. Other populations may well exist and attempts should be made to locate these.

Native Cymbidium
Cymbidium madidum

The long strap-like leaves and fragrant sprays of flowers or, more commonly, the large seed pods of this large epiphyte (**left**) are a familiar sight in rainforests and other moist habitats from the Hastings River in New South Wales to the tip of Cape York Peninsula. It grows in rainforests or, more commonly, in moist open forests from sea level to about 1500 metres in altitude. This species appears to do equally well in full sun or deep shade. The long, pendulous, sprays of fragrant flowers are borne in spring in the tropics. The flowers vary in colour from green through greenish-brown to yellow and last about two weeks. They are about two to three centimetres across. Inflorescences borne in the shade are usually longer than those borne in the sun. The plants often grow into huge specimens, in the forks of trees, in clumps of epiphytic ferns, on rotting logs or occasionally in leaf litter on the ground. Some of the largest plants seen by the authors were on mangroves on Hinchinbrook Island. When flowering has finished, the large shiny green, persistent seed pods are a feature of the plants.

The Native Cymbidium is a good species for pot cultivation, in a well drained, humus-rich mixture, tolerating a range of climatic conditions. Although it is collected from time to time, it is under no threat.

Cinnammon Orchid
Corymborkis veratrifolia

Often mistaken for a juvenile palm because of its pleated leaves, this terrestrial species of the rainforests grows to a height of about one metre. It occurs from the Whitsunday Islands to the tip of Cape York Peninsula and in New Guinea, Indonesia and South East Asia. It is a species of the densest, moistest lowland rainforests (or occasionally on the ranges), often near watercourses, growing in total shade with little air movement, but with high humidity and constantly warm to hot temperatures. The flowers (**left**) have a spicey perfume and are about two and a half centimetres across. They are borne in dense clusters of up to sixty, but commonly less, green and white flowers. Flowering occurs in the wet season (December to March).

The Cinnamon Orchid does not take well to transplanting, but once established does well in cultivation if given hot humid conditions and a rich soil. It is not under any threat, being quite abundant in the World Heritage Area and several national parks.

15

Dendrobium baileyi

Hot steamy lowland rainforests and mangroves are the habitat for this epiphytic species **(right)**. It has been recorded from Mount Elliot near Townsville to the McIlwraith Range on Cape York Peninsula, growing low down near major creeks and in the canopy, and occasionally at moderate altitudes. The plants flower throughout the year with an emphasis on the wet season. The flowers are about three centimetres across and are borne in groups of one to three at the nodes. Commonly known as one of the "one-day wonders" the flowers last less than a day before withering. The stems may be over a metre long, but are very slender and form dense clumps.

It is reasonably easy to grow on a slab, in a well drained pot or on a tree, but is intolerant of cold conditions. While this species is collected on occasions, it remains in good numbers in several national parks and is not considered to be under any threat.

Dendrobium luteocilium

The flowers of this large, robust epiphyte **(right)** are a little disappointing as they last only a day. It occurs from about the Tully River in the Wet Tropics of north Queensland to Iron Range on Cape York Peninsula and Moa Island in Torres Strait and New Guinea. It is a plant of the lowland rainforests growing high in the trees or on rockfaces where there is good light, high humidity and air movement. It also occurs in mangroves. The plants may grow to a large size with numerous stems up to two metres long. The flowers are about two centimetres across and are borne in bursts throughout the year with no distinct flowering season.

It does well in cultivation, but is not commonly grown due to the short-lived nature of the flowers. While it is not a common species, it is not considered to be under any threat.

16

Blue Orchid
Dendrobium nindii

The large showy flowers of the Blue Orchid **(left)** rate it as one of Australia's most attractive orchids. It is a rare species in Australia, having been recorded from about the Johnstone River to the Bloomfield River, the McIlwraith Range; and also in New Guinea. It is a species of the hot humid lowlands in high rainfall areas growing in mangroves, palm swamps and lowland gorges. Almost invariably it grows high in the trees in full sunlight, but often with the roots hidden in the shade of vines and other epiphytes. The flowers are large (up to six centimetres across) and long-lasting. The stems are up to one and a half metres long and are usually dark coloured.

Most collected plants do not survive, as the Blue Orchid is difficult to cultivate, although it does well tied to a tree in the Wet Tropics. It is now rated as vulnerable as it suffers from the twin threats of collecting and habitat clearing. Once relatively common in mangroves and palm swamps between Innisfail and the Bloomfield River, it is now hard to locate plants there, although some survive high in the treetops.

Mangrove Orchid
Dendrobium mirbelianum

This rather rare species **(left)** is readily mistaken for the more common Golden Orchid, but is quite distinct when in flower. It occurs in the hot steamy lowland swamps and mangrove forests from the Johnstone River to the Bloomfield River and in New Guinea, the Solomons and the Moluccas, usually growing high in the canopy where the light and air movement are good. The plants are usually smaller and more darkly coloured than the Golden Orchid, *Dendrobium discolor* (see page 7), and the flowers are not twisted. The flowering season is somewhat sporadic with an emphasis on spring. The flowers are long-lasting, are about four centimetres across, and there may be up to twelve on a raceme. The stems are commonly about thirty centimetres long, but can grow to a metre.

The Mangrove Orchid does well in cultivation in a pot, but requires consistent warm to hot conditions. It is regarded as endangered within Australia, due to the twin effects of habitat clearing and collecting. While it occurs in a few national parks, this is no guarantee of safety from collectors and it should be surveyed and a management strategy developed for it.

17

Swamp Orchid
Phaius tankervilleae

The Swamp Orchid is one of Australia's most sought after orchids. It is a robust terrestrial species which occurs from about Grafton in New South Wales to Cape York Peninsula, New Guinea, Indonesia, Malaysia and South East Asia. In the tropics it occurs from sea level to about 900 metres in altitude in open forests and rainforests in the coastal high rainfall areas. It always occurs in moist swampy conditions, where the soil stays moist throughout the year, often growing and flowering in deep shade which is prevalent in coastal melaleuca swamps, but sometimes growing in full sun in hillside soaks in open forest. The flowering season in the tropics is August to November, being earlier in the lowlands than on the tablelands. The spectacular flowers (left), which are about ten centimetres across, are borne on an inflorescence up to two metres tall, are long lasting and open progressively so that a plant is in flower for several weeks.

This species is readily grown in cultivation as long as it is kept evenly moist. It has been heavily collected in the wild, particularly in the southern part of its range where it also suffers from extensive habitat clearing and it is consequently rated as a vulnerable species.

Pomatocalpa macphersonii

This is an epiphyte of lowland rainforests from Rockhampton to the tip of Cape York Peninsula. It usually grows in shaded sheltered positions where there is little air movement. The plant consists of about five stiff leaves up to thirty centimetres long on a very short stem. The attractively-marked flowers are crowded at the end of a fleshy stem up to ten centimetres long and are about one centimetre across (opposite). Flowering is spasmodic throughout the year, with an emphasis on spring.

This species grows well in cultivation on a slab of hardwood or something similar or on a tree in the tropics. It is an abundant species and is not under any threat.

Eria kingii

This robust epiphyte (left) occurs from about the Tully River to Cooktown, the Iron Range and McIlwraith Range areas of Cape York Peninsula and New Guinea. It is a species of high rainfall rainforests, more common at low altitudes, but extending to about 800 metres in altitude, usually in areas of strong light. It also grows in moist open forests and on rockfaces. The flowers are about six millimetres across and are borne in spring (August to October). This species is better known under the old name of *Eria inornata*.

It is a good species in cultivation, doing well in a small pot of well drained medium, or on a tree in a tropical garden. It is not considered to be under any threat.

19

Tuberolabium papuanum

The Australian distribution of this small epiphyte is restricted to a small area in the Wet Tropics between about Innisfail and Cairns. It also occurs in New Guinea, the Solomons, New Caledonia and Fiji. It grows at low altitudes, on the outer twigs of rainforest trees overhanging creeks and in lowland gorges in areas of continuous high humidity. The attractive flowers **(right)** are about four millimetres across and are borne in progressive bursts along the fleshy inflorescence. The flowering season is February to April.

It does well in cultivation but is sensitive to cool temperatures and requires consistent high humidity. Although a rare species, it is not regarded as being under any threat, being well protected in the Palmerston and other national parks.

Giant Climbing Orchid
Pseudovanilla foliata

This climbing species occurs from north eastern New South Wales to the McIlwraith Range on Cape York Peninsula. It is a species of moist habitats, usually rainforests where it grows in decaying wood and leaf debris often on fallen logs or stumps. It is sometimes quite abundant in old logging operations and other places where disturbance has occurred, such as after a cyclone. It is a saprophytic species, deriving its supplies of food from fungus in the decaying wood. The brownish-green stems climb over the forest floor or over fallen logs and up the trunks of nearby trees sometimes to a height of twenty metres. The spectacular flowers **(opposite)** are produced in large masses, are sweetly scented and are about four centimetres across. They are borne from October to January.

Because of the saprophytic habit, this species is impossible to maintain in cultivation and should never be collected for this purpose. It is not considered to be under any threat.

White Bells
Sarcochilus tricalliatus

Although they take some finding, it is always rewarding to stumble on a colony of these plants with their crystalline white flowers **(right)**, in the harsh dry conditions of northern vine thickets in late spring. It is a small epiphyte which occurs from about Rockhampton to Princess Charlotte Bay on Cape York Peninsula. The glistening white flowers are about one centimetre across and are borne in November to January. This species grows on twigs at low altitudes in drier scrubs and vine thickets where there is strong light and good air movement. It is very closely related to Sarcochilus hillii which grows to the south.

It has proved to be difficult in cultivation and is best tied to a living tree. It may well be that small plants such as this have only a limited lifespan in any case and the habit of growing on small twigs may be a factor in this. It is locally abundant and is not considered to be under any threat.

Vrydagzynea paludosa

Little is known about this small, terrestrial species **(right)** which was discovered in Australia as recently as 1982. It has been recorded only once in Australia near the Daintree River in north Queensland, but also occurs in New Guinea. The habitat in north Queensland is lowland rainforest in deep shade and hot humid conditions with year-round rainfall. It grows in sandy soil with leaf litter. The flowering season is September and October and the flowers are about four millimetres long.

It is apparently relatively easy to grow if given hot humid conditions. It is rated as "vulnerable" as it is known from one site only and that site is private land and could be cleared in the future.

Tainia trinervis

There have been very few sightings of this small terrestrial species **(opposite).** This is probably because it is difficult to see, growing amongst dense undergrowth in lowland rainforest. The known range is between the Russell River and the Bloomfield River and in New Guinea, the Moluccas and the Solomons. The flowers are borne on a long spike and are about two centimetres across. Flowering occurs in spring (September to November). It is also known as *Tainia parviflora.*

It is readily grown in a shallow pot in an organically rich mixture, but is sensitive to cold conditions. Although rarely seen, this species is not regarded as threatened and it is not sought after by collectors. Populations are known in at least one national park.

Hairy Jewel Orchid
Zeuxine oblonga

The name "jewel orchids" is applied to this group because of the attractive sheen to the leaves. This is small terrestrial species of the rainforest floor **(right)** which occurs from northern New South Wales to the tip of Cape York Peninsula and in the northern part of the Northern Territory. It grows in leaf litter, often in fairly open rainforest conditions at various altitudes, but is more common in the lowlands, where it forms colonies. Individual plants grow to about twenty centimetres tall and are deciduous, losing their leaves in the drier part of the year. The flowers are small, about four to five millimetres across, and are borne in winter.

It is a common species under no threat and is relatively easy to grow in a shallow tray of leaf litter.

WET TROPICS
UPLAND OPEN FORESTS

The upland open forests occur on the western margins of the upland rainforests or occasionally on steep rocky or fire prone slopes. Although quite heavily logged for hardwoods, much of this type is otherwise intact as it is often on steep slopes or on soils which are not suited for agriculture. Much is reserved as State Forest. Along creeks there is often a line of rainforest trees and in areas not subject to violent floods, this is usually a good orchid habitat.

Perhaps the best orchid habitat within the upland open forest is the casuarina forest (right) which clothes many of the high misty ridges. These forests usually carry a heavy load of epiphytic ferns and orchids which are low down at eye-level in areas which have not been subject to heavy firing. Many of the species which are so dominant here also occur in the adjacent rainforests or on rock faces in the gorges of the mountain streams. These rock faces, particularly those near waterfalls, are a very prolific orchid habitat with large species such as the King Orchid, *Dendrobium speciosum* (see below), intermingling with tiny species such as Fairy Bells, *Sarcochilus ceciliae* (see page 32). The grassy understorey of these and eucalypt-dominated forests also provide a habitat for several species of terrestrial orchids such as species of *Diuris*, *Caladenia*, *Thelymitra* and *Pterostylis*.

Another rich habitat for terrestrial species occurs on the western slopes of the tableland where permanent springs provide ideal conditions for *Phaius*, *Spathoglottis*, *Habenaria* and *Peristylus* species.

King Orchid
Dendrobium speciosum

The King Orchid is one of Australia's most widespread epiphytes, occurring from Gippsland to Cooktown on the eastern Australian coast. In the tropics this species is more common growing on rocks than in trees. It grows in rainforest and open forest ranging from the harsh seasonally dry rocks west of the Dividing Range to the steamy rainforest of the lowland gorges and from 1500 metres altitude to sea level. Whatever the habitat, the plants will usually be found in areas of very strong light and good air movement. The flowers (page iii) are sweetly scented, white to yellow in colour and about three to five centimetres across (although this is very variable). They are borne in spring, July to August at lower elevations and September to October in the higher mountains. It is very variable and this has lead to several species being described, however the authors believe that the overall similarities and the presence of intermediate forms should result in these variations being considered as varieties at best.

The King Orchid is a very popular species in cultivation, and a number of different methods have proved successful. It is not regarded as threatened in Queensland, but it is collected widely and as it grows on rocks, it is vulnerable to over-collecting and it should be monitored in the future.

Spathoglottis paulinae

The striking purple flowers **(page 71)** of this endemic terrestrial species are a feature of swamp and stream margins in the Wet Tropics of north Queensland between a little south of Ingham to Cooktown. It occurs from about sea level to the tablelands, in open forests and swamp forests, always in areas of permanently moist soil. It often grows in company with the Swamp Orchid, *Phaius tankervilleae* (see page 19). The flowering season is July to March with an emphasis on spring (July to October) and the attractive flowers are about three centimetres across. In some forms the flowers are self-pollinating and do not open fully, but other forms open fully providing a fine display.

It grows readily in cultivation in a pot, if kept evenly moist. Although in demand by collectors, it is still present in good numbers and is not considered to be under threat although some monitoring of populations would be advantageous.

Pink Fingers
Caladenia carnea

The delightfully coloured delicate flowers of this orchid **(left above)** are a refreshing sight in the upland open forests in spring. It is a widespread species, occurring from Tasmania and south east Australia to the upland Queensland tropics, Indonesia and Malaysia. In the Wet Tropics it grows in grassy open forests at altitudes above about 500 metres, often forming scattered colonies. The flowers are borne singly or occasionally in pairs and are about two centimetres across. Flower colour ranges from deep pink through various shades to white. The flowering season is winter to spring (June to September).

Pink Fingers can be grown successfully in a well-drained mixture of sand and organic matter such as leaf mould. It is a common species under no threat.

Northern Bearded Orchid
Calochilus holtzei

This is one of the "bearded orchids", so named for the prominent hairs on the labellum **(left)**. It is a small terrestrial species from north Queensland, the Top End of the Northern Territory and northern parts of Western Australia. In north Queensland it has been recorded only a few times at moderate to higher altitudes on the ranges on the western margin of the Atherton Tableland, where it grows in tall grass in open forest. However it is a lowland plant in the Northern Territory and probably occurs on the coast in north Queensland also. The flowers are about two and a half centimetres across and last a day or two, however a plant will be in flower for a month or more as the flowers open progressively during the wet season.

Northern Bearded Orchids are difficult to maintain in cultivation for more than a year or two. In north Queensland this is a rare species, although the habitat of tall grass does make it difficult to locate. It does not appear to be under any threat.

Cypress Orchid
Dendrobium callitrophyllum

The Cypress Orchid is a small epiphyte which is restricted to the uplands of the Queensland Wet Tropics, occurring on the Windsor, Carbine, Atherton and Evelyn Tablelands. It occurs mostly on Cypress Trees, *Callitris macleayana*, in the tall open forests which grow on the western margins of the rainforests. It is also occasionally found in other scrubby trees on the rainforest edge. The flowering season is spring (August to October). The flowers **(right)** are about one and a half centimetres across and last about a week, changing colour as they age from greenish yellow to apricot. Surprisingly this distinctive species was described as recently as 1989.

The Cypress Orchid appears to be amenable to cultivation if grown in a cool climate. It is not an abundant species and part of the Evelyn Tableland population may be threatened by the proposed Tully-Millstream hydro-electricity project. Despite this the species is probably secure, although more data on abundance and distribution would be useful.

Leafy Hyacinth Orchid
Dipodium ensifolium

A large handsome terrestrial species occurring in north Queensland from about Ingham to the Daintree River, it is a plant of open forests of the moister regions. It is most tolerant of temperatures, occurring from sea level to the peak of Queensland's highest mountain Mount Bartle Frere. It grows in open eucalypt forests or in low heath usually in sandy soils. Underground there are long, fleshy, fragile roots which store water. The spectacularly-coloured flowers **(opposite)** are about two to three centimetres across, last a week or two and are borne in late spring.

In cultivation the Leafy Hyacinth Orchid often does well initially, then slowly goes backward and dies after a few years. It is closely related to the saprophytic *Dipodium* species such as the Hyacinth Orchid, *D. punctatum*, and may well be partly saprophytic itself. The lowland habitat is being cleared and this is placing pressure on some populations, but most highland sites are reasonably secure and the species is not in any immediate danger.

Chiloglottis longiclavata

A close inspection of the flowers of this small terrestrial species **(right)** will reveal a lip that is adorned with an insect-like callus which is involved in attracting the pollinator. It occurs above about 400 metres altitude from Townsville to Cooktown and grows in moist open forests and on rainforest margins, usually under grass or low bushes on well drained hillsides. The flowers are about two and a half centimetres long and the flowering season is April to June. This species was described as recently as 1990.

This species can be grown in an open, well-drained mixture. It is locally abundant and probably is more common than is thought as it is easily overlooked. It is not regarded as threatened.

Northern White Donkey's Tails
Diuris oporina

The small, but attractive, white to pale mauve flowers (**right**) of this terrestrial species are easily missed in the long grass of the mountain open forests in which it grows. The known habitat is the Atherton and Evelyn Tablelands, on the drier western slopes, but very similar plants have been reported as far south as the Paluma Range and Hervey's Range near Townsville. It is a small terrestrial, well adapted to the regular fires which sweep through the grassy open forest habitat. The main flowering season is April to July, possibly depending on fires, temperatures or rainfall. The flowers are about one and a half centimetres across and three to four centimetres long.

This species can be grown in cultivation, but requires some specialist knowledge. It is not regarded as threatened as large areas of the habitat remain intact.

Scented Sun Orchid
Thelymitra nuda

The Scented Sun Orchid (**opposite**) occurs in all states of Australia, growing on the ranges near the coast in the Queensland tropics, usually at altitudes of 500 metres or more, although it is occasionally reported at lower elevations. It grows in open forests in tall grass and while plants may be locally abundant they are widely spaced and are easily overlooked for this reason. The delicate blue flowers are about two centimetres across and open fully on sunny days only. The flowering season is August to October in the tropics. The plants survive the dry season as tubers under the ground.

It does well in cultivation if given a resting period and grown in a well-drained organically-rich mixture. It is not under any threat.

Dendrobium fellowsii

This small epiphyte is restricted to the mountain ranges from Paluma near Townsville to the Windsor Tableland. It occurs in moist open forests just outside the upland rainforests at altitudes above 800 metres in altitude. Some plants are high up in eucalypts, while others may be found lower in shrubby trees along creek banks. The interestingly-coloured flowers (**right**) are long-lasting, about two and a half centimetres across and pale green changing to light yellow with age. They are borne in summer from about October to January. Intense fires are a regular occurrence in the habitat and many older plants show evidence of being damaged by fire and recovering on several occasions. This species was previously well known as *Dendrobium bairdianum*.

This species is notoriously difficult to grow, and it is not recommended for cultivation. It is not considered to be under any threat.

Peristylus banfieldii

Apart from the original collection by the famous naturalist Edmund Banfield ("the Beachcomber") on Dunk Island in 1906, the only other known records of this terrestrial species are from near Cardwell and near Mareeba on the Atherton Tableland. Here it grows beside soaks which flow out from under the basalt cap and provide a perennially wet environment. The plants (right) stand about half a metre tall when in flower. The new leaves appear at the onset of the wet season in January, and the flowers follow a few weeks later, dying back to an underground tuber at the end of the wet in about June. The flowers are about one centimetre across and an inflorescence lasts about a month.

This species does well in cultivation if grown in a sandy open mix, but needs a dry resting period. The conservation status is not clear as this species has so rarely been seen. Possibly it is safely conserved in the Dunk Island National Park, but it has not been recorded in the last eighty years. The habitat at Mareeba is not conserved, but is under no threat.

Northern Yellow Donkey's Tails
Diuris luteola

In early spring the beautiful yellow flowers (opposite) of this dainty terrestrial species can be found in upland grassy open forests. It has been recorded from the Carnarvon Range, Blackdown Tableland, Paluma Range and the Atherton Tableland, always in the moderate to high altitude open forests adjacent to high rainfall areas. It usually grows in long grass on hillsides and ridges in stoney soils and the bright yellow flowers, about two and a half centimetres across, are a feature of this country in early spring (July to September). The habitat is subject to regular fires in October to December and the plants are well adapted, surviving as tubers to grow again in the wet season.

Northern Yellow Donkey's Tails can be grown in cultivation, but is not popular as specialist conditions are required. As the habitat is rarely cleared and the species is in several national parks, it is not considered to be under any threat.

Tall Greenhood
Pterostylis stricta

A colony-forming terrestrial (right), this
species is quite abundant on the ranges and
tablelands of the Wet Tropics of north Queensland
between about Paluma and Cooktown. It grows in
sheltered conditions in denser open forests and
rainforest margins. As with all other Greenhoods,
the lip is capable of sudden motion, being triggered
by a potential pollinator alighting. This effectively
traps the insect which, in escaping, pushes past the
stigma, either receiving pollen on its back or
depositing pollen on the stigma. The flowers are
about two to three centimetres long and the flowering
season is autumn.
   It is readily grown in a pot in an organically rich
but well-drained mix. It is not regarded as threatened.

Fairy Bells
Sarcochilus ceciliae

The dainty pink flowers of this small lithophyte
always seem to be out of place on the dry, harsh rock
faces on which it grows (opposite above). It occurs
from about the Hastings River in New South Wales to
the Atherton Tableland in north Queensland. In the
northern part of its range it grows above altitudes of
about 300 metres in areas of unfiltered light and
extreme temperatures in the middle of the day. The
leaves are heavily pigmented and are fleshy to store
water and avoid desiccation in this harshest of
habitats. The thick roots form an extensive system
seeking out any crevices in the rocks where a little
moisture may remain. The delicate flowers are about
six millimetres across and are borne in October to
December.
   Fairy Bells is a good subject for cultivation, doing
well in a shallow dish with a perfectly-drained
compost. It is not considered to be under any threat
in north Queensland, although some populations
have been heavily collected.

Charging Bull Orchid
Pterostylis taurus

Dense colonies of this attractive small terrestrial
species are a feature of open forests and rock ledges
in north-eastern Queensland from the Whitsunday
Islands to the Windsor Tableland (opposite below).
The name derives from the resemblance to a bull,
with the sepals representing the horns. The plants
grow in large colonies at low to moderate altitudes,
usually at the base of rocks where there is a little extra
moisture retained in the soil. The flowering season
is May to July and a large colony in full flower is a
magnificent sight. Each flower is about one and a
half centimetres across. After flowering the leaves
gradually wither as the dry season takes hold.
During the dry season the plants survive as
underground tubers. New leaves are produced with
the coming of the wet season.
   The Charging Bull Orchid does well in
cultivation, provided it is given the correct
conditions and is given a rest during the dry season.
It is a locally abundant species under no threat.

WET TROPICS UPLAND RAINFORESTS

Between Townsville and Cooktown high mountains occur close to the sea and much of the rugged range country above about 500 m is clothed in upland rainforest, with cloud forests on the highest ridges and peaks in exposed situations above 1000m. The two types intergrade and share many species. In the cloud forests **(right)** there is virtually continuous high humidity, good air movement, cool temperatures and periods of good light alternating with cloudy conditions. Branches are covered with mosses and other small epiphytes including numerous orchids. The upland rainforests of the Wet Tropics are largely intact with the important exception of the Atherton Tableland area where the rainforests on basalt soils have been reduced to remnants by clearing for agriculture and dairy farming. Where the rainforests occur on flat or gently undulating country there are few orchids, but along the streams and on the margins of clearings and open forests the conditions allow more light penetration and air movement and orchids abound. For this reason the small remnant patches which remain on the tableland are doubly important for orchid conservation.

In the canopy large epiphytes occur on the larger trunks or in forks, but the real diversity is often in the small branches of the outer canopy where tiny species of *Bulbophyllum*, *Taeniophyllum* and other genera occur. On the forest floor terrestrial species such as the jewel orchids with their attractive leaves may be abundant in areas where there are rocks, or on slopes where the drainage is good, or on the banks of small streams.

Apricot Orchid
Dendrobium fleckeri

The green to cream or apricot coloured flowers **(lower right of front cover)** of this small species are a feature of the cool, misty peaks of the Wet Tropics of north Queensland in spring. This species may be quite abundant on the higher peaks such as Mount Bartle Frere, Mount Lewis and Thornton Peak, rarely occurring below 1000 metres altitude. It occasionally grows on rainforest trees but is more common on rocks where there is good light and air movement. It freely produces aerial growths, and can form large patches, rather like the familar Pink Rock Orchid, *Dendrobium kingianum* does further south. A few flowers can be found at most times of the year, although the main flowering time is spring and early summer. The flowers are about three centimetres across, sweetly scented, and are distinctive in the hairy labellum.

It is not recommended for cultivation other than in situations where cool moist conditions are available. While the habitat is limited, there are no clearing pressures on the mountain tops and as the species is not commonly collected, it is regarded as secure.

Oak Orchid
Dendrobium jonesii

The fragrant white sprays of the Oak Orchid
(**page i**) are a feature of mountain forests in spring
throughout the Wet Tropics. It is a widespread and
locally abundant species in coastal tropical
Queensland from Mount Elliot near Townsville to
the Pascoe River on Cape York Peninsula. While this
spectacular species occasionally occurs at sea level
it is primarily a species of the moist mountain ranges
where it grows in rainforest, but is also at home in
the tall open forests fringing the rainforests. The
flowering season is spring, from about August to
October, and the flowers, while lasting only about
a week, are fragrant. There are several forms of the
Oak Orchid including the large-flowered variety
magnificum which has flowers up to five
centimetres across.

In cultivation the Oak Orchid does well in
cooler areas. This species is heavily collected,
but is still in large numbers and is not considered
to be under any threat.

Bulbophyllum evasum

The interesting globular head of flowers
(**left above**) which this small species produces is
unique among Australian orchids. It is a small
creeping epiphyte of the cloud forests between the
Paluma Range and the Bloomfield River south of
Cooktown. The habitat is very moist, mossy
rainforests generally above 1000 metres in altitude
where there is constant high humidity, air
movement and alternate periods of strong light
and mist. The plant can grow into dense mats
of long brittle stems on mossy branches or rocks.
The flowers are tiny (about three millimetres across)
but are borne in a dense globular head about one
centimetre in diameter. Flowering may take place
at almost any time of the year, with a peak
in late spring.

This species is not easy to establish in
cultivation and should not be tried if the material is
to be gained by collecting in the wild. It is locally
abundant and is not under any threat as the
mountain top habitat is rarely disturbed.

Jewel Orchid
Anoectochilus yatesiae

This is one of a number of so called "jewel
orchids", named for the attractive, distinctively-
patterned leaves (**left**) which have a jewel-like
appearance when the light strikes them. It is
restricted to the upland rainforests of the Wet
Tropics of north Queensland from the Paluma
Range to about the Bloomfield River where it
occurs in dense rainforests always in shady
conditions and often near water, such as on
stream banks. The flowers are small (about fifteen
millimetres long) and relatively unattractive.

It can be grown successfully if given cool,
humid, shady conditions. Although occasionally
collected, this species is not at risk as it is difficult
to locate and many populations exist in remote parts
of the rainforest.

Bulbophyllum lageniforme

This small epiphyte is one of the many species of *Bulbophyllum* occurring in the Wet Tropics. It is found in cloud forests between about Innisfail and Cooktown, almost always at altitudes above 900 metres where it grows in cool misty, humid situations on trees or rocks where there is good air movement. In these conditions it is often locally abundant. The flowering season is November to February and the flowers are about eight millimetres long. The flattened pseudobulbs are produced close together on the rhizome like a string of beads **(right)**. This species and those appearing on this and the following page are typical of this large, variable genus. Often the true beauty of these small species is not evident at a glance and requires the use of a lens to appreciate the delicate colours and structures.

It is not an easy species to grow and should only be tried in cooler climates. It is not regarded as under any threat as the habitat is virtually never cleared.

Bulbophyllum lewisense

Named after Mount Lewis where it was first discovered, this is a small pendulous epiphyte **(right)** of upland areas of the north Queensland Wet Tropics. It has been recorded on Mount Lewis, Carbine Tableland and the Windsor Tableland at altitudes of 900 to 1200 metres. It prefers the smaller branches of rainforest trees in cloudy, misty conditions and grows into small, pendulous clumps of stems up to fifteen centimetres long. The flowers are about five millimetres long and are borne in September to October. The small size and habit of growing high in the canopy of tall rainforest trees resulted in this species being unknown to science until 1979 when it was collected during the course of work on the classification of rainforest trees by one of the authors of this book.

This species is not well known in cultivation, but some plants have been grown successfully at Atherton. The range is probably not fully established as yet, as it is only seen when a rainforest tree comes down, but it appears to be under no threat from clearing or collecting.

Bulbophyllum lilianiae

This miniature species **(left)** is restricted to upland areas of the Wet Tropics, growing in cool, moist cloud forests above 1000 metres in altitude. The plant consists of thin, thread-like creeping strands of pseudobulbs each about one centimetre long, with about one centimetre between them. They grow over outer tree branches and twigs in areas of good light, high humidity and good air movement. Plants only occasionally occur on rocks. There are usually two flowers, each one centimetre across on a spike about two centimetres tall. The delicate flowers are pale red with three darker stripes on the segments. The main flowering season is spring (July to September).

This species is difficult to grow in cultivation as the cloud forest conditions are not readily reproduced in the bush house. It is a reasonably common species and is not under any threat as the habitat is never cleared and it is not popular with collectors.

Bulbophyllum sladeanum

This miniature epiphyte is restricted to the Atherton, Evelyn, Windsor and Carbine Tablelands, Mount Lewis and adjacent ranges. It occurs in rainforests at higher altitudes, usually above 800 metres, forming small, dense clumps on twigs of trees in moister forests where the humidity is high **(left)**. While flowering may occur at almost any time, there is an emphasis on autumn and winter. The flowers are about two centimetres across and are often abundant on a large plant, being borne singly on a flowering stem up to seven centimetres long. There is some debate as to the status of this plant, with some authorities regarding it as a species and some considering it as a variety of *Bulbophyllum macphersonii* (variety *spathulatum*).

Although a miniature, this is a popular plant in cultivation as it is free-flowering and relatively easy to grow, doing well on a slab in humid conditions. It is not regarded as being under any threat.

Cadetia taylori

The dense mats **(right)** of this species are a
common sight covering tree trunks and rocks
in the upland areas of north Queensland. It is a small
species of the rainforests from Mount Elliot near
Townsville to Iron Range and New Guinea. It is more
common at higher altitudes, but also occurs at sea
level and is usually more abundant in shaded
conditions, but in areas of good air movement.
Occasionally in the mountains, it completely covers
large rocks in the rainforest. When this occurs the
glistening white flowers, which are borne in
profusion, make quite a spectacle. The flowering
season is rather spasmodic with an emphasis on
summer. The flowers are about one centimetre
across and last several weeks.

It does well in cultivation in a well drained
medium, but should be kept moist. It is an abundant
species in the Wet Tropics and is not under
any threat.

Nodding Helmet Orchid
Corybas abellianus

The small attractively-patterned leaves of this
species **(right)** are rarely seen, being well hidden by
leaf litter and rainforest undergrowth. It is a tiny
terrestrial of the rainforests of the Atherton and
Evelyn Tablelands and possibly also the McIlwraith
Range. It occurs at altitudes of 700 metres and above.
It grows in shaded, sheltered, moist environments
usually of rainforests or rainforest margins, where
it can form large colonies. The plant consists of an
underground tuber and a single leaf which is absent
during the dry season in winter and spring. The
single flower is about five millimetres long and
is borne in the wet season.

The Nodding Helmet Orchid has been tried in
cultivation and has proved difficult. It appears not
to be common but, as it is easily overlooked, this
is not certain. As the habitat is not being cleared,
it is not considered to be under any threat.

Dendrobium lichenastrum var. *prenticei*

This orchid **(left)** is a small epiphyte
or lithophyte which occurs from Mount Elliot near
Townsville to about Cooktown. It grows from sea
level to 1000 metres in altitude, in rainforests or in
moister open forests where it forms mats on rocks
or tree branches, usually in areas of good light and air
movement. The flowers are about five millimetres
across and are borne throughout the year. There is
considerable debate over the naming of this species
as it is very variable in leaf size and shape and it has
been described as a species – *Dendrobium prenticei*.
The flowers are, however, identical with those of
Dendrobium lichenastrum (see page 41) and varietal
status would seem appropriate.

It is an excellent species for cultivation, growing
well on a slab in a range of climates. It is not
considered to be endangered in any way.

Christmas Orchid
Calanthe triplicata

The spectacular tall sprays of white flowers
of the Christmas Orchid **(left)** form a spectacular
display in the mountain rainforests of the
Wet Tropics in December. It is a large terrestrial
species which has a very wide distribution, ranging
from Madagascar through Asia to New Guinea.
In Australia it occurs from southern New South
Wales to the Iron Range area on Cape York Peninsula.
It grows in rainforests and occasionally in moist open
forests in areas where there is a build up of leaf debris
and the drainage is good, such as between rocks.
In the tropics it is more common at moderate to high
altitudes. It often grows into large clumps and in
colonies which are very obvious due to the large
pleated leaves from half to almost a metre long.
The flowering spikes are borne from October to
January and are even more obvious, standing up to
one and a half metres tall and bearing numerous long-
lasting flowers each about three centimetres across.

It is a relatively easy species to grow in a well
drained, organically-rich medium. While this species
is not listed as rare or threatened, it has been heavily
collected in some southern parts of its range and
populations should be monitored.

Buttercup Orchid
Dendrobium
agrostophyllum

A walk on any of the moist high ridges of the
northern ranges in spring is likely to uncover the
bright yellow flowers (right) of the Buttercup Orchid
adorning the thick windswept vegetation. It is an
attractive species which is restricted to the Wet
Tropics area of north Queensland, where it occurs in
the cooler, misty highlands from Mount Elliot (just
south of Townsville) to Cooktown. It is equally at
home in rainforest and open forest and is tolerant
of strong sun or shade. The flowers are about one
centimetre across and are produced on small plants
low down in the vegetation or even growing in the
leaf litter. On the other hand large plants with
numerous canes up to sixty centimetres long are a
feature of some exposed granite rocks on Mount
Bartle Frere and Mount Lewis. It is also particularly
common on casuarina trees in the moist open forests
which occur adjacent to the mountain rainforests
in areas such as Wallaman Falls.

The Buttercup Orchid is difficult to cultivate in
warm climates and really should not be tried unless
cool, moist conditions can be provided. It occurs
in large numbers and is not considered to be under
any threat.

Dendrobium carrii

This small creeping epiphyte (right) is restricted
to the Atherton Tableland and other upland areas
north to about the Annan River. It grows on outer
branches of trees in upland cloud forests where there
is always moisture and good air movement and
where misty cloudy conditions are common. The
flowers are about one and a half centimetres across
and are borne in spring (August to October) on a stem
of about five to ten flowers. Large plants can cover
tree limbs with a tangled mass of stems, but it is more
common as long slender stems with well-spaced
pseudobulbs each with a pair of leaves.

Although rarely grown, this species does
reasonably well in cooler climates if given the correct
conditions and a slab to grow on. It is not considered
to be under any threat.

Dendrobium adae

The delicate, fragrant cream to green flowers
(**left**) of this slender epiphyte adorn the upland
rainforests from Mount Elliot near Townsville
to Mount Finnigan near Cooktown. It is restricted
to relatively high altitude rainforests above about
800 metres in altitude and is almost always
epiphytic, but in contrast to most epiphytes seems
to prefer shady situations. In some highland areas
such as Paluma, it may be a very abundant orchid
and, as it often grows low down on tree trunks, it is
one that is often seen by visitors, particularly in the
flowering season in spring (July to October). The
flowers are about two to two and a half centimetres
across and are variable in colour, ranging from white
to cream or light green or apricot and tending to
darken with age. They are strongly perfumed.
The pseudobulbs grow up to sixty centimetres,
but a length of around twenty to thirty centimetres
is more common.

This species is quite amenable to cultivation in
cooler areas such as the southern states, but should
not be attempted in the tropical lowlands. It is an
abundant species and is not considered to be under
any threat.

Dendrobium lichenastrum var. lichenastrum

The dense clumps of small fleshy leaves of this
species (**left**) are a fairly common sight in the upland
rainforests from the Eungella Range near Mackay to
about the Daintree River. It grows at moderate
altitudes, usually above 600 metres, in rainforests or
in moister open forests where it forms mats on rocks
or tree branches, usually in areas of good light and air
movement. The flowers are about five millimetres
across and are borne throughout the year. There is
considerable debate over the naming of this species
as it is very variable in leaf size and shape. Forms
with long, cylindrical leaves have been variously
described as species, varieties or forms. The most
common form is known as *Dendrobium lichenastrum*
var *prenticei* or *Dendrobium prenticei* (see page 39).

It is an excellent species for cultivation,
growing well on a slab in a range of climates.
It is not considered to be endangered in any way.

Leafless Nodding Orchid
Epipogium roseum

The delicate, white stems and flowers of this saprophytic species (**right**) are rarely seen, partly because it is rare, but largely because it is visible above ground for a period of a few days only while the flowers grow, open and then produce seed. It is a widespread species being recorded from northern New South Wales to the tip of Cape York Peninsula, New Guinea, South East Asia, Japan, India and Africa. In the tropics it grows at a range of altitudes and habitats, but is most common in rainforest. During most of the year the plants exist underground, obtaining food from symbiotic fungi in the soil. The flowering stem is produced in the wet season and may be up to sixty centimetres tall with numerous flowers each about one and a half centimetres long.

It should never be collected for cultivation as the saprophytic lifeform renders it impossible to grow. It is not considered to be under any threat.

Northern Tangle Orchid
Plectorrhiza brevilabris

The untidy spreading root system of this and other related species have lead to the name Tangle Orchid. It is a pendulous epiphyte of the small trees and shrubs and occasionally in the canopy and on rainforest margins from south-eastern Queensland to the McIlwraith range on Cape York Peninsula. In the tropics it is an upland species, growing above about 500 metres in altitude, while further south it grows in the lowlands. The plants are commonly eight to fifteen centimetres long and the flowers, which are borne on an inflorescence about five to fifteen centimetres long, are about one centimetre across. The flowering season is November to February. While the individual flowers are not spectacular, a large plant in flower (**opposite**) can be quite striking.

The Northern Tangle Orchid is well suited to cultivation, doing well on a slab in a bush house or on a tree in a protected position. It is a relatively abundant species and is not considered to be under any threat.

Phreatia baileyana

The small, succulent leaves of this species (**right**) are quite common in the Wet Tropics, but are rarely seen and rarely recognised as an orchid. It occurs from the Paluma Range to about Cooktown, growing at moderately high altitudes in rainforests and moist open forests. Occasionally it grows on fallen trees, appearing to thrive in these conditions and often forming large colonies from seedlings. It appears to favour trees with a rough or stringy, moisture-retaining bark. The flowers are tiny, about one and a half millimetres across and the flowering season is late spring.

It grows well in cultivation on a slab which retains some moisture and should be kept in humid conditions. It is not collected in significant numbers and is not considered to be under any threat.

Eulophia zollingeri

This species is a saprophyte and most records are from rainforest in shady conditions, usually near rotting stumps. It has been recorded from the Atherton Tableland and the Cooktown area, but also occurs in New Guinea, Indonesia, South East Asia and India. In Australia it has been recorded at low altitudes, but is apparently more common above 700 metres in altitude. As it is a saprophyte and lacks leaves, it is easily overlooked except for the period when the flowers are above ground. The strikingly-coloured flowers **(right)** are large, about six centimetres across and are borne on a stem up to ninety centimetres tall. Flowering occurs during the wet season in summer.

Cultivation is not possible as it is a saprophyte and plants should never be collected. It is rare, but is not considered to be under any threat.

Tableland Pencil Orchid
Dendrobium racemosum

One of the Pencil Orchids, so named because of the long cylindrical leaves, this species is abundant in mountain rainforests on the Atherton Tableland, Evelyn Tableland and some nearby areas on the lower Russell and Johnstone Rivers. It is primarily a species of the tablelands, where it grows on rainforest trees particularly on forest margins in areas of persistent misty rain and good air movement. It often colonises street trees in Tableland towns. The long branched stems are initially erect, becoming pendulous as they lengthen. The slender flowers **(opposite above)** are about two and a half centimetres across and are borne throughout the year, with an emphasis on spring.

The Tableland Pencil Orchid does well in cultivation if grown on a tree or a slab in cooler climates. It is locally abundant and is not considered to be under any threat.

Sarcochilus serrulatus

This small epiphyte occurs on the Atherton and Evelyn Tablelands and the Mount Lewis area, in higher altitude areas above 800 metres. It occurs in the dense highland vegetation, often along creek banks where it may be locally abundant. In these localities there are constantly humid conditions, reasonable to low light and little air movement. The plants are only a few centimetres across and the attractively-coloured flowers are about one and a half centimetres diameter **(opposite below)**. The flowering season is mostly spring and summer. It is closely related to, and often grows with, *Sarcochilus olivaceus*, but can be distinguished by its minutely serrate leaves and the brick-red flowers.

This species does well in cultivation, but requires a cool climate and humid conditions. It is not regarded as being under any threat.

CAPE YORK PENINSULA OPEN FORESTS

Cape York Peninsula lies in a different biogeographical zone to the Wet Tropics south of Cooktown. Most of the Peninsula is strongly seasonal with a most pronounced dry season from May to December and a shorter, but reliable, wet season from December to April. The open forests, woodlands and monsoon scrubs or deciduous vine thickets occupy the seasonal areas – in effect about 90% of the Peninsula.

Only one very hardy epiphytic orchid grows in the eucalypt-dominated open forests, while the melaleuca woodlands are host to only a few more. Conditions are very harsh in these habitats with high temperatures even in mid-winter and full sunlight for days on end. Regular dry season fires are also a constant environmental factor in these areas. A few terrestrial species survive by retreating to underground tubers during the dry, then producing leaves and flowers during the wet.

The vine thickets (see page 2) are sensitive to fire and grow in areas where fire cannot penetrate such as rocky hillsides where the abundant surface rocks do not allow the growth of sufficient grass to carry a fire; or on beach dunes or on stream banks. Such thickets are only a little more friendly than the open forests as they tend to lose all, or a good part of, their leaf cover during the dry in response to water stress **(right)**. The Cooktown Orchid, *Dendrobium bigibbum* (see below and page 47), most spectacular of Australia's orchids, thrives in these vine thickets along with a few other hardy species.

Cooktown Orchid
Dendrobium bigibbum var. *superbum*

This variety of the Cooktown Orchid **(upper right of front cover)** occurs south of the Archer River on Cape York Peninsula. It is abundant in scrubby habitats where fire cannot penetrate, such as patches of monsoon forest on stony soil which cannot support a dense grass cover, and in beach scrubs, gallery forest lining small streams and occasionally on rock faces. On the Peninsula the wet season stretches from the early storms of December through the driving rains of January to March to the lighter showers of April. After this comes the monotonous dry heat of the northern winter and spring when conditions are hard and harsh and the leaves fall from the trees of the monsoon forests. The spectacular flowers are up to seven centimetres in diameter and are long-lasting. The flowering season is at the end of the wet season in about February to May.

The Cooktown Orchid does well in cultivation if the basic requirements of a dry resting period in winter and spring and hot temperatures can be provided. The popularity of this species in horticulture has lead to heavy collecting in the wild, most of it illegal as almost all of the habitat is Crown leasehold land on which this species is protected. Large populations still survive on Cape York Peninsula, but unless collecting stops the long term future is not secure.

Cooktown Orchid
(northern form)
Dendrobium bigibbum
var. *bigibbum*

The Cooktown Orchid is one of the great horticultural species of the world. The long-lasting sprays of pink to purple flowers are born in autumn at the end of the northern Australian wet season. This is a variable species and over the years several varieties and even species have been recognised. The most distinctive varieties are: variety *bigibbum* (**left**) with smaller flowers, often with a white spot on the lip. This occurs north of the Archer River. Variety *superbum* (see page 46) has larger flowers and occurs south of the Archer to about Mount Molloy. Variety *compactum* (see page 4) is a small-growing form of the coastal ranges south of Mossman. In all forms occasional pure white plants are found. The northern form of the Cooktown Orchid occurs on the northern part of Cape York Peninsula, and on the islands of Torres Strait and southern New Guinea. It is particularly common in vine scrubs behind the beaches and on rocky hillsides. The climate is strongly seasonal, although the rainfall is reliable, it all falls in the period from January to April, with a pronounced dry period during winter and spring. The habitats in which this species grows are not noted for retaining a humid atmosphere during the winter, so that this species has to cope with long dry periods. The flowers are about four centimetres across – a little smaller than those of the other varieties but the shape, colour and markings, as well as the long arching inflorescences which contain many flowers, ensures that this is a very attractive variety for cultivation. The flowering season is February to May and the flowers last for several weeks. A recent publication has elevated the three varieties mentioned above to the status of species, but the authors of this book consider that this is not warranted.

To be successfully grown it must be kept warm and dry during winter and spring and must be well drained. It does well attached firmly to a tree in a tropical or sub-tropical garden. It has been heavily collected in the wild, particularly from some Torres Strait Islands, and is regarded as vulnerable.

Dendrobium canaliculatum x Dendrobium trilamellatum

This naturally-occurring hybrid between the Tea Tree Orchid, *Dendrobium canaliculatum* (see page 9) and the Yellow Antelope Orchid, *Dendrobium trilamellatum* (see below) has been reported a few times from various locations on Cape York Peninsula but appears to be more common on the islands of Torres Strait. Being a hybrid there is a great deal of variability, but all are intermediate between the two parents. The plants grow in the harsh seasonal melaleuca forests which are the habitat of both parents. The flowers **(right)** are variable, but are generally about three centimetres across and are long-lasting. The flowering season is spring (August to November).

Like many hybrids, these plants are relatively easy to grow, if the habitat conditions are kept in mind. Hybrids such as this are rare and are attractive to collectors, but are likely to keep occurring as long as populations of both parents grow in proximity.

Yellow Antelope Orchid
Dendrobium trilamellatum

This robust epiphyte **(opposite)** thrives in habitats in which few other orchids can survive. It occurs from a little south of Cooktown to the islands of Torres Strait, southern New Guinea and the Top End of the Northern Territory. It is a species of the very seasonal and hot open melaleuca woodlands where the wet season usually starts in December with occasional storms building to heavy rain in January to March, followed by a dry season in which virtually no rain falls from June to November. The Yellow Antelope Orchid flowers in spring (July to September) and the flowers are attractive, long-lasting and pleasantly scented. They are about three to four centimetres across.

In cultivation this species does moderately well, but must be given a dry season and the medium must be well drained. There is some collecting pressure on this species, but it is not regarded as under threat at present.

Pink Tea Tree Orchid
Dendrobium carronii

This colourful miniature species **(right)** was named as recently as 1982. It is closely related to the more common Tea Tree Orchid, *Dendrobium canaliculatum* (see page 9) from which it differs in the flower colour and the smaller petals. The distribution is eastern Cape York Peninsula, Torres Strait and southern New Guinea. On the Peninsula it grows in moister eastern areas usually on paperbarks or on trees of the gallery forests or hillside scrubs. Often the spray of attractive flowers is larger than the plant, being up to two and a half centimetres across.

Although this is a colourful and most attractive species, it is not recommended for horticulture as it has proved difficult to keep alive for more than a year or two. It is currently not under any threat, although increased collecting which could follow on improved access to the Peninsula may cause problems in the future.

Nervilia holochila

Colonies consisting of hundreds or even thousands of the single erect light-green leaves of this seasonal terrestrial species are a common sight in the coastal open forests of tropical Australia. It occurs in eastern and northern Australia from about Mackay to Cape York Peninsula, across the Top End of the Northern Territory to the Kimberleys, also the islands of Torres Strait and New Guinea. The delicate flowers **(right)** are about one and a half to two centimetres across and appear in November or December after the first soaking rains of the wet season. The leaves **(right below)** appear as the wet season gets into full swing and remain well into the dry season.

This species is quite amenable to cultivation, provided it is given a resting period from about May to October with little or no water. It is under no serious threats from collecting or land clearing.

Curly Pink
Dendrobium x superbiens

One of Australia's most spectacular orchids this is actually a naturally-occurring hybrid between the Cooktown Orchid, *Dendrobium bigibbum* (see page 47) and the Golden Orchid, *Dendrobium discolor* (see page 7). It is known from the tip of Cape York Peninsula and the islands of Torres Strait. It occurs occasionally where both parents are growing nearby and in one or two places may even be locally abundant. The parents seem to be quite interfertile, but the hybrid is rare because they flower at different times of the year. Curly Pink is a year-round flowerer and the flowers are long-lasting and up to five centimetres across **(opposite above)**.

This is a hardy species and does well on a tree in many north Queensland gardens or in a bush house further south. It has been heavily collected particularly from the Torres Strait Islands and should be regarded as vulnerable.

Brown Antelope Orchid
Dendrobium johannis

The Brown Antelope Orchid **(opposite below)** is an epiphyte of open forests on eastern Cape York Peninsula from the Stewart River to the islands of Torres Strait and southern New Guinea. It grows at low altitudes in moist open forests and rainforest margins, rarely being found in true rainforest, as it seems to prefer well-lit situations with good air movement. This species rarely grows into a large plant and most are relatively small, with stems to about twenty centimetres long. The interestingly-coloured, long-lasting flowers are about two centimetres across and are usually borne in autumn, but some from the northern part of the range tend to flower in spring.

It is quite a good specimen in horticulture and does well in the tropics tied to a tree. This species is locally abundant, but is collected heavily, particularly where it grows near roads and is under some pressure, although it would be premature to rate it as vulnerable.

Saccolabiopsis armitii

Dry, semi-deciduous scrubs and thickets of north-eastern Queensland are the habitat of this small epiphyte **(right)**. It has been recorded from sea level to moderate altitudes from near Bundaberg to northern Cape York Peninsula, and probably also from New Guinea. The range extends from coastal scrubs up to two hundred and fifty kilometres inland and the habitat can be extremely harsh in the prolonged dry season from May to December. The flowers are crowded on the inflorescence, with up to fifty small flowers each about four millimetres across. The flowering season is September to December.

This species is hard to maintain in cultivation on a long term basis, but does best tied to a slab in a brightly-lit situation. It is not considered to be under any threat.

New Guinea Ground Orchid
Spathoglottis plicata

This is a large, showy, terrestrial species confined in Australia to Cape York Peninsula. Overseas it is widespread in the Pacific, New Guinea, and South East Asia. The long broad leaves are a feature of swamp margins, hillside soaks and creek banks on Cape York Peninsula. The flower spike appears in spring and may be over one metre tall. The flowers **(opposite)** are about three centimetres across, opening progressively so that the plant is in flower for a month or more. All the Australian plants seen have purple flowers, but specimens from overseas vary in colour from purple to white. One of the world's most popular horticultural species, it is commonly used as a garden plant in wet tropical areas such as Cairns and Singapore.

In cultivation it requires a well-drained position, but needs to be kept moist year round. In the wild the populations are reasonably secure as the remote nature of many habitats deters collectors as does the relative abundance of the species in cultivation.

Habenaria elongata

This small terrestrial species has been recorded from only a few locations in coastal Queensland from Rockhampton to the tip of Cape York Peninsula, the Top End of the Northern Territory, the northern part of Western Australia and in New Guinea. It grows most commonly in open forests in the monsoonal regions, but has also been recorded from exposed headlands in low grassy areas. In the dry season the plants lose their leaves and survive as tubers under the ground, with new leaves appearing in response to the early rains in December. The flower spike **(right)** stands erect to about fifty centimetres with numerous flowers about two centimetres long, opening over a period of about a month. The flowering season is January to March.

It does well in cultivation if given a dry resting period from May to December. The plants are secure as their habitat is rarely cleared and they are not in demand by collectors.

CAPE YORK PENINSULA RAINFORESTS

The Cape York Peninsula rainforests occupy those areas on the east coast where there is a winter component to the rainfall. Most of the Peninsula is extremely seasonal, but in a few areas such as the Iron Range area, the McIlwraith Range, the headwaters of the Jardine River and the Bamaga-Lockerbie area the topography leads to a regular dry season rainfall, ranging from substantial in the McIlwraith Range to a light misting sufficient only to maintain humidity levels in the Jardine area. These rainforests (right) are mostly at low altitude, although the McIlwraith Range reaches an altitude of just under 1000 metres.

Orchid numbers are high, with both terrestrials and epiphytes being present in good numbers and surprising diversity, particularly along streams and on rockfaces and the rock piles of Tozer's Gap. There is a strong New Guinea influence in these rainforests with several species which are common in New Guinea having an outlying occurrence at Iron Range or the McIlwraith Range. The Tozer's Gap rockpiles are granite boulders some as large as a small house stacked on one another in a wild jumble. There are few trees as only a few figs can survive the soilless conditions, but it is an excellent habitat for epiphytes, the rocks offering conditions quite similar to the canopy of the rainforest. Contrasting to this are the gallery forests of the larger streams which support some of the most beautiful rainforest in Australia, although the orchids here are far out of sight in the canopy.

Bulbophyllum blumei

This species (lower left of front cover) is an epiphyte occurring in the Jardine River area of Cape York Peninsula and on Moa Island in Torres Strait and from New Guinea to Malaysia. On Moa Island it grows in a very dense, moist, rainforest at about 400 metres altitude, while on the Peninsula it grows at low altitudes in rainforest or occasionally in heath areas. It often grows into large clumps, covering entire limbs of rainforest trees, seen here on the right hand tree. The flowering is spasmodic throughout the year with an emphasis on winter. The flowers are about seven centimetres long and last a few days.

It does well in cultivation in a basket or on a slab, but is not tolerant of low temperatures. Although it is occasionally collected, it is under no threat.

Rhinerrhiza moorei

This species occurs in the Iron Range and McIlwraith Ranges of Cape York Peninsula and in New Guinea and the Solomon Islands. It grows in lowland rainforest usually low down on the tree trunks in deep shade and in conditions of high humidity and low air movement, although it can tolerate bright light. The flowers (page 1) are about one and a half centimetres across, lasting for less than a day. They are borne on a very long inflorescence, which produces progressive bursts of flowering.

Plants do well in cultivation, but are vulnerable to low temperatures. Although collected occasionally, this species is relatively secure.

Cape York Vanda
Vanda hindsii

This robust species grows equally well on trees or rocks in the McIlwraith Range and Iron Range areas on Cape York Peninsula and in New Guinea. In Australia it grows in lowland areas where the rainfall is high and the dry season is not too pronounced. The spectacular long-lasting flowers are about three centimetres across and can occur at any time throughout the year, but the emphasis is on late spring and summer. Occasional yellow-flowered forms have been reported, but most are an enamel brown **(upper left of front cover)**. The rock faces on which this species grows into large clumps in the Iron Range area are extremely hot at the end of the dry season and the root system spreads out for metres from the plant seeking access to any available moisture.

It is a good subject for cultivation, provided it can be given hot temperatures and perfect drainage. Some populations have been depleted by collectors and this species should be regarded as vulnerable.

Dendrobium bifalce

One of the more common species in lowland New Guinea, this large epiphyte or lithophyte occurs on the islands of Torres Strait and Cape York Peninsula south to the Daintree River. It is a plant of the wet tropical lowlands growing equally well on rocks or trees, usually in areas of strong light and good air movement. It often grows into large clumps and flowers freely, producing attractive long-lasting colourful flowers **(left above)** about two to three centimetres across. In localities such as Iron Range, it is an abundant species, although the casual observer may not be aware of this as most specimens are high in the trees or on inaccessible rockfaces.

In cultivation this species grows readily in areas well south of its habitat but often refuses to flower there. In coastal north Queensland it will grow and flower on a tree in the garden. Although collected on occasions, it is not considered to be under any threat.

Coconut Orchid
Dendrobium litorale

This slender epiphyte has been recorded in Australian territory only once – on Duaun Island in Torres Strait. It is an abundant species in lowland New Guinea. On Duaun Island it grows on trees in patches of rainforest on granite rockpiles at an altitude of about two hundred metres. The plant produces aerial growths prolifically and grows into dense clumps up to fifty centimetres long. The flowers **(left)** are about one centimetre across and last a few days. The flowering is spasmodic throughout the year.

It does well in cultivation, tied to a tree or in a pot of fern peat or something similar. Although rare in Australia, this species is not under any threat as the habitat will never be cleared and as it is an abundant species in New Guinea.

Antelope Orchid
Dendrobium antennatum

This is a common species in lowland New Guinea. In Australia it is rare, occuring only in the McIlwraith Range in lowland gorge situations with good air flow and strong sunlight. There is no set flowering season and the delicately-coloured flowers **(right)**, which are about four centimetres across, are very long-lasting. A large plant may have flowers for much of the year.

The Antelope Orchid is a popular species with orchid growers, growing well in bushhouses in tropical and subtropical areas. It is under pressure from collectors and is considered to be vulnerable.

Graceful Orchid
Bulbophyllum gracillimum

This small epiphyte is widespread outside Australia, occuring from South East Asia to New Caledonia, but has been recorded in Australia on only one or two occasions from the Iron Range area on Cape York Peninsula. There it grows in low tangled rainforest vegetation on ridges of low to moderate altitude. The individual flowers are about three centimetres long with very fine segments and are grouped into a head of about six to ten flowers **(opposite above)**. The flowering season is spasmodic throughout the year.

This species does well in cultivation in a pot or on a slab, but must be kept warm throughout the year. This species is listed as "rare" and the numbers in Australia should be monitored as it is a popular species for collectors.

Bulbophyllum longiflorum

This attractive epiphyte is one of the world's most widespread orchids. Within Australia it occurs in the McIlwraith and Iron Range areas of Cape York Peninsula while it also is widespread in Africa, South East Asia and the Pacific Islands. On the Peninsula it grows in dense rainforest at moderate elevations in shaded areas where there is good air movement and high humidity. The flowers are about four centimetres long **(opposite below)** and the flowering period is summer and autumn and the flowers last about a week.

In cultivation it does well in a basket or on a slab if given warm conditions. The Australian populations are rated as vulnerable as this is a desirable species and is sought after by collectors.

Cadetia wariana

This is a small mat-forming plant **(right)** of trees or rock faces in the McIlwraith and Iron Ranges of Cape York Peninsula, Moa Island in Torres Strait and New Guinea. It occurs at low to moderate altitude in rainforest or moist open forest, often in semi-shaded positions. The glistening white flowers are about six millimetres across and are produced in numbers. The plants are also shiny and the overall effect is a very attractive miniature orchid.

This species does well on a slab. It is not under any threat as the habitat is never cleared and the species is rarely collected.

Spider Orchid
Dendrobium tetragonum var. *giganteum*

The distinctive four-angled stems of the Spider Orchid are a feature of the scrubs of the east coast of Australia from southern New South Wales to the Iron Range area of Cape York Peninsula. The variety *giganteum* occurs north from about Mackay. Generally it grows in mountain rainforests, always on trees, often near watercourses. The spider-like flowers (**right**) can be up to ten centimetres long and very attractively marked. The flowers last about a week and a large plant covered in flowers is a spectacular sight. The Spider Orchid is a variable species and some authorities consider the large-flowered form shown here to be a separate species, *Dendrobium capitisyork.*

It responds well to cultivation on a tree or on a slab in tropical and subtropical areas. This species is abundant in certain areas and is under no immediate threat.

Dendrobium insigne

Lowland New Guinea is the major habitat of this epiphytic species which has been recorded from Saibai Island and doubtfully from Cape York Peninsula. It is a species of the hot steamy lowland rainforests, sometimes growing in mangroves. The stems grow to nearly half a metre. The flowers (**opposite**) are about three to four centimetres across and last about two days. They are borne in bursts sporadically throughout the year. This is one of a few species which occur commonly in New Guinea and "overflow" to the islands of Torres Strait and northern Cape York Peninsula.

It is easy to grow, provided it is not exposed to cold temperatures. It is rare in Australian territory, but a relatively common species in New Guinea and is not considered to be threatened.

Dendrobium tetrodon

The slender pendulous leafless stems of this species are a familiar sight in the gallery forests lining Cape York Peninsula streams from about the Stuart River to Cape York. It also occurs in Indonesia. It grows at low to moderate altitudes usually in rainforest, monsoon thickets and gallery forests. In many of these habitats there is a pronounced dry season during winter, spring and early summer. This species is deciduous during the dry months and produces new growths and flowers during the wet season in summer and autumn. The flowers last about a week and some do not open fully, presumably being self-pollinating. When they do open, the flowers are about two centimetres across (**right**). It was previously well known in Australia as *Dendrobium stuartii.*

It is a good subject for cultivation if grown on a slab and kept away from cold temperatures. It is collected occasionally, but is not considered to be under any threat.

Brittle Climbing Orchid
Dipodium pictum

This species occurs at Iron Range and the McIlwraith Range on Cape York Peninsula and in New Guinea. It is a species of rainforests at low to moderate altitude and climbs on trees or rocks, often near creek banks in shady, humid conditions. While the plants start terrestrially, they often die off in the older parts, leaving the remaining plant as an epiphyte. The stems are brittle and it is not unusual for fragments of plants to be snapped off and start a new plant on the forest floor. The attractive flowers **(right)** are about four centimetres across and are borne at almost any time of the year with an emphasis on spring.

This species does well in cultivation as long as it is kept warm and grown on a slab on which there is room for it to climb. This is not a common species and, as it is sought after by collectors, population numbers should be monitored.

Hoop Pine Orchid
Dendrobium wassellii

Hoop Pines, *Araucaria cunninghamii,* in the McIlwraith Range and Cape York area on Cape York Peninsula are almost the sole habitat of this small creeping epiphyte **(opposite)**. It occasionally grows on other tree species and on rock faces, but the particular bark conditions and the high light of the upper branches of the Hoop Pines seem to suit this species best. It grows from a little above sea level to about 700 metres altitude. The flowers are about two and a half centimetres across and last about a week. The flowering season is from about April to June.

In cultivation the Hoop Pine Orchid does very well at least as far south as Brisbane on a slab or on a tree. It is not under significant collecting pressure as it grows high in the trees in a remote area.

Tozer Range Orchid
Dendrobium tozerensis

This slender epiphyte or lithophyte remained unknown to science until the authors of this book discovered it at Iron Range in 1975. It is restricted to the Iron Range – McIlwraith Range area of Cape York Peninsula. It grows at low altitudes in high rainfall areas usually on trees or rocks where light and air movement are at high levels such as on rocks near creeks and waterfalls or on scattered trees on rockpiles. The flowers last only a day, are borne throughout the year and are about three to four centimetres across **(right)**.

The Tozer Range Orchid does well in cultivation on a slab, but probably would be intolerant of low temperatures. The remote nature of the habitat is good protection for this species, but as it is not in large numbers it has been rated as vulnerable.

Flickingeria comata

Within Australia this species is distinctive because of the branched erect or semi-erect stems which can grow to sixty centimetres long. This is a robust epiphyte or lithophyte which occurs in the McIlwraith and Iron Range areas of Cape York Peninsula and in New Guinea, Indonesia and South East Asia. It is a species of lowland rainforests on trees or rocks in sheltered rather than exposed positions. The weirdly-shaped flowers are about two to three centimetres across and have a densely-fringed apex to the lip **(right)**. They are borne in profusion on a large plant, but last less than one day. Flowering occurs sporadically throughout the year.

This species does well in cultivation as long as it is given warm conditions, but few plants have found their way into collections. It is occasionally collected, but is not considered to be threatened.

Rainforest
Habenaria
Habenaria hymenophylla

This terrestrial species has been recorded from a few localities in north Queensland between Townsville and the tip of Cape York Peninsula and in the Top End of the Northern Territory. It grows at low altitudes in moister monsoon forest and rainforest margins. The leaves appear after the first soaking rains of the wet season in December or January and the flowers follow soon after, lasting for about a month in flower as new flowers open. The flowers **(right)** are about one centimetre across and are borne on a stem up to almost half a metre tall. The rosette of leaves lasts well into the dry season, eventually dying back to an underground tuber.

The Rainforest Habenaria does well in cultivation if grown in a rich, well-drained mixture and given a dry resting period in winter and spring. Although rare, it is not regarded as being under any threat.

Luisia teretifolia

This long slender epiphyte occurs from about Mossman to the tip of Cape York Peninsula, the Top End of the Northern Territory, New Guinea, Indonesia and South East Asia. In Australia it occurs in hot, humid lowland situations such as swamp forests, mangroves, rainforest margins and moister open forests. It prefers situations of good light and air movement. The plants grow into tangled, pendulous clumps up to forty centimetres long. The flowers are about one centimetre across and are usually poorly displayed, being bent in towards the stem (left). The main flowering period is during summer (November to March).

It does well in cultivation, but must be given perfect drainage and is best tied to a slab or tree in the tropics. Although it is occasionally collected and some of the habitat has been cleared in the southern-most part of the range, it is still present in good numbers on Cape York Peninsula and is not considered to be under any threat.

Malaxis marsupichila

The glossy green leaves of this terrestrial species (left) are a feature of the Cape York Peninsula rainforests in the wet season and it is surprising that it was not discovered until 1976. It is an abundant species in the better-drained shady sites in the monsoon rainforests of the Peninsula from about the Stewart River to the tip of the Cape. It has also been discovered at one locality in the Northern Territory. The attractive leaves are deciduous, being absent from about June to December. When the leaves are missing, the plants are almost impossible to locate as they are usually covered by the deep leaf litter present at that time of year. The leaves quickly grow after the first soaking rains and the long spikes of small flowers follow soon after. The flowers may be purple or green and are about eight millimetres in diameter.

It is easy to grow in cultivation if given the necessary rest period. It is under no threats, other than being occasionally dug up by wild pigs.

63

Oberonia complanata

This epiphytic species which ranges from northern New South Wales up the east coast of Australia to New Guinea, tolerates a wide range of habitats from sea level to 1000 metres altitude. It grows in exposed or shaded conditions on trees or rocks and in open forests, rainforests and mangroves, but does best in bright sunny conditions where the plants take on a yellowish colour **(right)**. The individual flowers are tiny, only about two millimetres across, but are very numerous on the inflorescence. They are borne throughout the year with a concentration on spring (August to October).

It does well in cultivation, although it is only rarely tried, doing best on a slab or in a small pot of coarse mix. It is not under any threat.

Harlequin Orchid
Sarcochilus hirticalcar

The McIlwraith Range on Cape York Peninsula is the only area from which this small epiphyte **(opposite)** is known. It grows at low to moderate altitudes and can be locally abundant in the gallery forest along small streams. It grows low down on small branches or on the flaky bark of the Hoop Pines, *Araucaria cunninghamii*, and has also been reported on the flaky-barked Red Beech, *Dillenia alata*, on floodplains on the east coast of the Range. The flowering time is October to December and the plant is in flower for several weeks as the flowers open progressively. The interestingly-marked flowers are about one centimetre across.

The Harlequin Orchid is well suited to cultivation on a slab. Due to the apparent rarity and the attraction of this plant to collectors, it has been rated as vulnerable.

Tuberolabium stellatum

This epiphytic species **(right)** is endemic to the Iron Range – McIlwraith Range area of Cape York Peninsula. It grows in rainforest at moderate altitudes, in areas which may experience a reasonably distinct dry season, but remain humid throughout the year. It is closely related to *Tuberolobium speciosum* (see page 66), but can be distinguished by the semi-pendulous leaves. The delightfully-coloured flowers are about one centimetre across and are borne in successive bursts on the fleshy inflorescence. The flowering season is not well known, but appears to be throughout summer. In the habitat, it is occasionally locally abundant but is not often seen as it grows high in the rainforest trees.

It does well in cultivation, but will not withstand cold temperatures. It is not regarded as being under any threat, but is collected on occasions.

Pomatocalpa marsupiale

This large, robust epiphyte has been recorded only a few times in Australia in the McIlwraith Range – Iron Range area of Cape York Peninsula. It also occurs in New Guinea, Bougainville Island and the Solomons. It is a species of rainforest at low to moderate elevations, growing high in the canopy or occasionally on exposed rocks. The flowers are about one and a half centimetres across, with a pouched lip (hence the name "marsupiale") and are borne in a dense head on a branched inflorescence **(right)**. Flowering usually begins in about November and continues to about April, with flowers opening progressively.

It is readily grown in cultivation in a large pot of open mixture, or tied to a tree in the tropics. It is a rare species and is sought after by some collectors, but the habit of growing high in the canopy and the remote nature of the habitat provides good protection and it is probably not under any threat in Australia.

Tuberolabium speciosum

The flowers of this epiphytic species last only a day or two but on a large plant they are produced prolifically, creating a spectacular display **(right)**. It occurs in the rainforests of the Iron Range – McIlwraith Range area of Cape York Peninsula where it grows at low to moderate altitudes often on rainforest margins or on Hoop Pines, in areas where there is a distinct dry season. It is closely related to *Tuberolabium stellatum* (see page 64), but can be distinguished by its erect leaves. The flowers are about twelve millimetres across and are borne in progressive bursts on the fleshy inflorescence. The plants flower sporadically throughout the year, with an emphasis on summer.

This species is amenable to cultivation, but is susceptible to cold conditions and requires good drainage. It is locally abundant and, while it is sought after by collectors, it is not considered to be under any threat.

Trichoglottis australiensis

This epiphytic species is restricted to the McIlwraith Range and the Iron Range area on Cape York Peninsula, where it grows on rainforest trees and occasionally on rockfaces, usually in conditions of low light and high humidity at altitudes of about 300 to 700 metres. The pendulous stems are up to forty-five centimetres long and it can grow into a large, branched plant. The brightly-coloured flowers (left) are about one and a half centimetres across and are borne on a short inflorescence of two to six flowers. The flowering season is autumn (March to June).

This species is amenable to cultivation, but will not stand cold temperatures. Because of its habit, it is best suited to culture on a slab. It is locally abundant and, while plants are occasionally collected, it is not considered to be under threat.

Robiquetia wassellii

This small to moderate-sized, pendulous epiphyte from the McIlwraith Range to Iron Range area of Cape York Peninsula occurs in shaded, humid environments, often growing low down on trees in rainforests at low to moderate altitudes. It can grow into a sizeable clump with stems up to forty centimetres long, but most plants are small. The flowers (page 68) are about one and a half centimetres long and are borne in a dense raceme about ten centimetres long. They last a week or two and are produced in spring (August to October). This species was discovered in the late 1960s and was named after the late Lea Wassell, a noted bushman and collector from Coen.

In cultivation, this species is best grown on a slab in a warm, humid situation. It is a restricted species, although it is often abundant locally. There is some collecting pressure on it, but it is considered to be relatively secure, being well protected by the Iron Range National Park and the proposed McIlwraith Range Park.

Robiquetia wassellii

Further Reading

AUSTRALASIAN NATIVE ORCHID SOCIETY 1963 - present	The Orchadian. A quarterly journal. Vols. 1 - 10
CLEMENTS, M.A. 1989	Catalogue of Australian Orchidaceae. Australian Orchid Foundation & Reed, Melbourne
DOCKRILL, A.W. 1969	Australian Indigenous Orchids. Society for Growing Australian Plants, Sydney
JONES, D.L. 1988	Native Orchids of Australia. Reed, Sydney
DRESSLER, R.L. 1981	The Orchids: Natural History and Classification. Harvard University Press, Cambridge, Massachusetts.
LAVARACK, P.S. & GRAY, B. 1985	Tropical Orchids of Australia. Nelson, Melbourne
NICHOLLS, W.H. 1969	Orchids of Australia – the Complete Edition. Nelson, Melbourne.
ORCHID SOCIETY OF NEW SOUTH WALES. 1936 - present	Australian Orchid Review. A quarterly journal. Vols. 1 - 57
THOMAS, M.B. & MCDONALD, W.J.F. 1989	Rare and Threatened Plants of Queensland. 2nd Edition. Dept. Primary Industries, Brisbane.

Photographic Credits

(abbreviations following page numbers are : a = above, b = below)

BRUCE GRAY:	front cover, i, ii, 4, 5b, 7, 8a, 9a, 10b, 11a & b, 12, 13a & b, 14a & b, 15b, 16a & b, 17a & b, 20a, 21, 22a & b, 23, 24, 25b, 26a & b, 27, 28a & b, 29, 30, 31, 32, 34, 35a &b, 36a & b, 37a & b, 38a & b, 39a & b, 40a & b, 41a & b, 42a & b, 44, 45b, 47, 48a & b, 49, 50b, 51b, 52a & b, 54, 55b, 57a & b, 58a & b, 59, 60a, 61, 62a & b, 63a & b, 65, 66a & b, 67, 68
BILL LAVARACK:	1, 3, 6b, 8b, 10a, 19a & b, 20b, 25a, 33a & b, 46, 50a, 51a, 53, 56a & b, 60b, 64a & b, 71, back cover
CLIFF & DAWN FRITH:	iii, 5a, 6a, 9b, 15a, 43, 45a, 55a
G.A.WOOD/A.N.T. PHOTO LIBRARY:	18

Typesetting & Finished Artwork by Law Design Pty Ltd   Printed by Inprint Limited, Australia

Index to Orchids

(Page numbers in boldface are those subjects illustrated)
(fc = front cover; bc = back cover)